making holy
dreams come true

a book of prayers and meditations by
Garth Hewitt

photographs by
Wilf Whitty

for Orla May,

Sabelo Samora

and Harley Jonah

First published in Great Britain in 2006

Society for Promoting Christian Knowledge
36 Causton Street
London SW1P 4ST

British Library Cataloguing-in-Publication Data
A catalogue record for this book is available from the British Library

ISBN-13: 978—0—281—05857—0
ISBN-10: 0—281—05857—1

1 3 5 7 9 10 8 6 4 2

Designed and typeset by Theresa Maynard
Printed in China on behalf of Compass Press Limited

contents

garth's introduction

This is a book of prayers and meditations illustrated with Wilf Whitty's photos. I have wanted to write some daily prayers for some time and I have added prayers for special occasions, and prayers that focus on issues around the world; these were born out of journeys to Amos Trust partners.

At Amos Trust, we have a commitment to four areas of the world in which we have projects: South Africa, where we support Umthombo — a project working with street children; India, where we support work with a Dalit community (Dalits were formally known as 'outcastes'); Nicaragua, where we support a school in a very poor area; and the Holy Land, where we support a hospital in Gaza and a conflict resolution centre in Bethlehem, as well as reconciliation work and a pre-school nursery in Israel.

For more information about these projects, do visit our website at www.amostrust.org or contact us at Amos Trust, All Hallows on the Wall, 83 London Wall, London EC2M 5ND; phone: 020 7588 2661.

Wilf Whitty is the designer for Amos Trust and he has travelled with me to some of our projects — his photos reflect these visits. I love the way he often photographs the unexpected, or has an eye for the design in the unusual, or finds humour in the unlikely place. I think that with prayers it is important not simply to say the words, but also to be still for a while. Wilf's photos allow a quiet moment of meditation or reflection — so thank you, Wilf.

As the book was coming together, I helped lead a retreat with St Paul's Cathedral Institute, and a talk by Canon Lucy Winkett inspired two or three ideas that ended up in the prayers — so thank you Lucy.

I thought of the prayers and meditations as primarily for personal use, perhaps as a daily prayer book for people travelling. Some are suitable for use in communal worship as they were written for our liturgies for Wednesdays on the Wall held at All Hallows on the Wall, City of London, or for Thursdays at the Gate held at the Westgate Chapel in Lewes, East Sussex.

For more information on these services go to www.allhallowsonthewall.org

Garth Hewitt

chapter 1

---

daily prayers

sunday morning

In the quiet I come to you
I find strength to start anew
Breathing out and breathing in
In the quiet I come to you

I find stillness in the storm
Despite the struggles all around
A sabbath rest — take time to pause
In the stillness I come home

In the dawn I come to you
Past the piper's haunting tune
Morning creeping from the east
In the dawn I come to you

You raise my head — you lift my heart
Every day another start
You meet us in the simple things
In the quiet where we begin

In the quiet I come to you
I find strength to start anew
Breathing out and breathing in
In the quiet I come to you

sunday evening

Thank you for today — a break from the normal —
Maybe it has been quiet and restful
Or full of exercise and enjoying creation
Or a day with family and friends —
A day to worship and remind ourselves
Of the character of a loving God.

My father used to say
'The battle for the day is won the night before'
And maybe we are now ready —
And perhaps nervous, about tomorrow.

Give us a good night's sleep — a restful night.
We place into your hands those we love
May we wake refreshed —
Good night.

monday morning

Gracious and loving God — I pause before the rush —
Before I check the traffic news.
There are tasks to be done today —
May I reflect your values and attitudes
Even though it may be very busy
May I have time for people.
Fill me with your joy for today
That I go out invigorated
To lift people up — to be a bringer of hope
Confident in your love
Realistic and wise in the difficult moments
Light of spirit and a friend to laughter
Sensitive — one who listens
And one who knows when to say 'enough' and to rest.
I commit myself into your hands for all that must be done today
In the name of God — creator, redeemer and sustainer.

monday evening

Evening time I come to you
As the busy day is through
In the warmth of evening light
I bow my head — I come to you

At the ending of the day
I lay it down — I lay it down
All that I have done this day
I lay it down — I lay it down

May the quiet be my friend
Tomorrow I can start again
So I put my hand into God's good hand
Refreshing sleep — come again

Stars are shining bright tonight
I lay it down — I lay it down
What's done is done — put it aside
I lay it down — I lay it down

Evening time I come to you
As the busy day is through
In the warmth of evening light
I bow my head — I come to you

tuesday morning

Keep me observant today, God
Observant of your world
May I hear birdsong
See trees and flowers
Look for animals
Enjoy the beauty of the world —
Commit myself to action when I see it spoiled
May I never take it for granted

And may I remember friends today
Especially those who need my prayers
Especially the old who will think of me
Especially those who are ill

Keep my spirit fresh and my heart joyful
In the name of God — creator, healer and hope bringer

tuesday evening

It is time to say good night
I lay it down — I lay it down
There are things still left undone
I lay it down — I lay it down

The wind that murmurs in the trees
The gentle lapping of the sea
The earth itself seems at peace
It's time for busy thoughts to cease

I give it into God's good hands
I lay it down — I lay it down
Still my soul and still my mind
I lay it down — I lay it down

The wind that murmurs in the trees
The gentle lapping of the sea
The earth itself seems at peace
It's time for busy thoughts to cease

Evening time I come to you
As the busy day is through
In the warmth of evening light
I bow my head — I come to you

wednesday morning

God of community and compassion
This morning I take a moment to look round the world
At the needs of those who do not have enough to eat —
And those who cannot break the chains of poverty
Those who try to survive on the streets of the cities of our world.
I pray for politicians that they will remember
The weak and the vulnerable
For those who work to bring hope to the vulnerable —
For campaigners, those who give and those who pray.

Gustavo Gutiérrez said 'Woe to those the Lord finds dry-eyed'
Keep our hearts warm, Lord, and our vision clear and simple
That we play our part for the healing of the worldwide community —
It may seem such a small part
But it is something beautiful for God.
And now as we go out to serve you in our community
We commit to you all we will meet
In the name of God the compassionate, the merciful and the just.

Wednesday evening

Loving God, thank you for this day —
Thank you for the opportunities
For the people I met — for the people on my mind
I'm sorry for the mistakes and the wasted opportunities
But I look forward to tomorrow — a fresh start

May I be grateful for each day and each friend
For each moment of laughter
For each burst of song
For each sight of beauty in creation
For each generous human trait

May I treasure it all
And may this night's sleep renew me
I love the quiet at the ending of the day
It is a healing restoring moment
To quieten the mind
Ready for sleep
Good night, God, good night

thursday morning

Prayer is like sunbathing — says Rowan Williams —
How wonderful and you don't even need sunscreen!
How liberating and what a generous understanding of God —
That we can pause in God's presence
Breathe deeply and find we are restored.

Today may we find time to pause
And have 'little sabbaths' of refreshment
Where we are renewed
As we remember the character of this loving God.
May we say the names of those on our mind —
And say no more —
But lift them in our minds into the hands
Of this restoring, generous God.
Today do a little sunbathing
And feel the difference.

thursday evening

You're the One, you're the Living One
You're the truth against the false
You're the friend of the poor
And you tear down the walls
You are the living God.

You break the walls of hatred — of prejudice and greed
You heal the broken-hearted — restore the ones in need
You're power to the powerless — hope to the weak
You are the prince of peace.

You're not like the God of money — you're not like the God of war
You were born into a stable — you live beside the poor
The price is not all that matters to you
People mean so much more.

So teach us to be like you, Lord, and tear false idols down
To bring the light of the gospel wherever the dark is found
Your kingdom brings hope to a world torn apart
May we show your love today.

You're the One, you're the Living One
You're the truth against the false
You're the friend of the poor
And you tear down the walls
You are the living God.

friday morning

God of life, teach me to listen —
To know your protest over exploitation
To feel your pain over the tearing of the fabric of life and community
As the poor get poorer and the rich get richer.
I have heard the poor speak of their misery —
Of feeling the pain in their flesh — of their hunger
Of not being able to get healthcare for their children
So they die of easily curable diseases.
I have stood with the young man whose wife died in childbirth
Because the proper care was not available.

God of life, teach me to listen —
It is not enough to say 'We didn't know'
Or to say 'When did we see you hungry?'
You are the God who says 'Do it to the least'.
Never has our world known such wealth — such skills —
Such healthcare — such education
Yet . . . such inequalities.

Future generations will ask 'Why were you silent?'
God of protest at exploitation and misuse of resources
Can we claim to be followers — if we do not listen —
If we do not raise our voices — if we do not protest?
Lord, give us your compassionate heart
And take not your spirit of protest from us.
Lord, help us to remember and take up the cross of caring
And take not your spirit of protest from us.

friday evening

God our companion, we are restless
Until we find our rest in you
You were with us at our beginning —
And we are rootless . . .
Until we find our roots in you —
So may we make time to pause . . .
And meet you in the silence.

You are the oasis of mercy where souls are restored
You walk beside us — you make us whole
You are the rhythm of life — the rhythm of our souls
We find, in the rhythm of prayer, that you meet us
Lifting us up, day after day — giving us strength.

It is in the taking of 'little sabbaths' that our souls catch up
We often intuitively know when they can't catch up —
Teach us to wait and pause and be silent
For silence is the place that restores us —
It is the place of preparation for all that is to come —
It is the still small voice.

God our companion — oasis of mercy
You still move in mysterious ways
You are the cloud of unknowing
But you meet us in the silence.

saturday morning

Today, Lord, I would like to give thanks for family and friends —
To bring them into your presence
And ask you to surround them with your love.
I will name them
And then take time to be quiet for a while . . .
All the hopes and all the fears
All the joys and all the worries
Of those close to me I bring to you.
The old ones who have done so much for us over the years —
We remember them and are grateful
The young ones full of life, energy and fun —
We thank you for them
And the way they move us and make us laugh.
You are the God who laughs with us and weeps with us
Don't let us rush too much today —
But rather may we pause and cherish those we love
And do activities that refresh and restore us.

God of all of life —
Thank you for the Saturday lie-in
For the late morning brunch
For the afternoon sport or leisurely walk
For the concert or cinema trip
For pottering in the garden
For the takeaway and the DVD
For the good book or favourite CD
God of all life — restore us on this Saturday Sabbath.

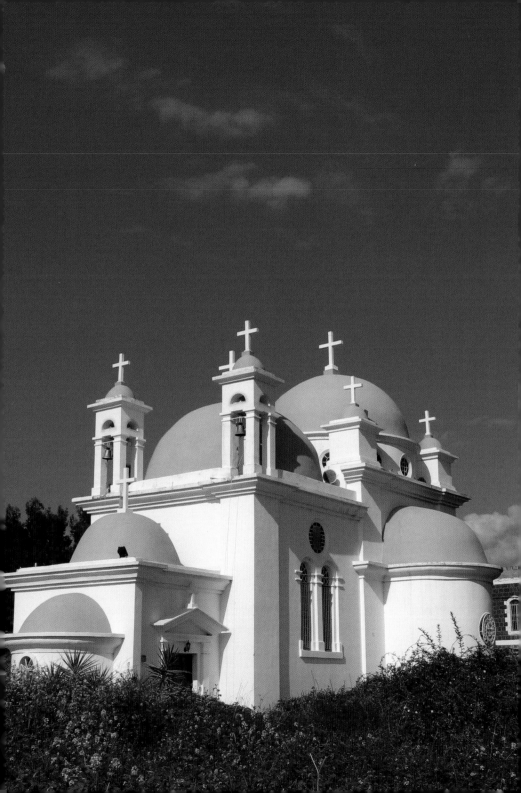

saturday evening

God, I thank you for today —
Now as I turn to rest
My thoughts turn to tomorrow
Normally a day to worship —
A day of Communion or Eucharist —
The banquet of joy and peace —
The meal of justice
The moment when heaven meets earth —
Where time meets eternity
A meal where bread and wine are transformed
And so should we be — into people of compassion.

I do not often feel the excitement of all this potential . . . to be honest
But I need to be reminded of the values of your community
To be reminded that this vulnerable and flawed community
Has wisdom that our world needs to hear
I need to come off the throne of my life
And allow the values of the Sermon on the Mount to permeate me
I need to meet you and allow you to serve me —
May tomorrow inspire and motivate
And give me a hint of what can be
If only we live out your values.

chapter 2

---

prayers around the world

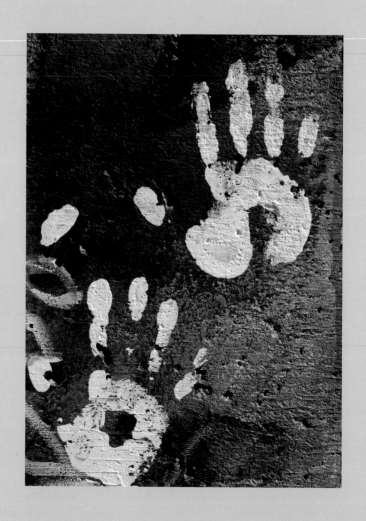

prayer for south african street children

Compassionate God
May we be those who listen to the voices of the
    forgotten generation —
The children on the streets of South Africa.
Day by day they face the challenges of abuse,
    hunger and trauma
Always asking 'will anyone care for me?'
God of mercy and justice, may we reach out in love
As we remember that each day is a battle —
Each day is a struggle to survive.
Bless the work of those who walk beside them
As they seek daily to bring strength, dignity
And hope for these forgotten children.
May the children of the streets — walking the road
    to crucifixion —
Find the way to resurrection —
Because we listen — because we support them
And because we bring your holy and active love.
We ask in the name of Jesus
Who said 'let the children come to me'.

meditation in durban, south africa

Loving God —
I visited a township today curiously called '85 Palmeit'
It is in an area called Sydenham —
But not like the Sydenham I know.

16,000 to 20,000 people are living here in a shanty town —
On the side of a steep hill — heading down to the river.
It was very difficult even to walk from house to house —
In rain it would be impossible.
The sewage ran down the middle of the camp.
I was told there is one tap for all these people
And shown four green plastic toilets for the whole community.
How can this be?
In a town that has just said it will spend
Over a billion rand on the World Cup in 2010?

I asked how many are unemployed in the township —
I was told it was over 90 per cent.
I met a girl who had to beg on the streets when she was seven —
To try to survive — now she is nine and her family have been helped
And are now able to keep her off the streets.

But this is why there are street kids — because they are growing up
In places with no facilities, no healthcare —
They cannot afford education — their parents cannot get jobs.

85 palmeit

Opposite 85 Palmeit are huge houses —
Further up the road are some of the smartest mansions one could
  ever see —
Also a very fancy shopping mall.
An international cricket match is happening down the road
But 85 Palmeit is hidden from the sports fans.
The motorway goes right past —
It appears that nobody cares
For 85 Palmeit and the many, many places like it.

O God, I visited a township today —
I won't forget it —
I don't know how they survive at all.
Thank you for those who do come and try to bring some help —
To try to stop more children from ending up on the streets.
But help us all to remember
That 'no one is free until all are free'.

An apartheid of poverty still exists.
There is a task to be done —
Loving God, don't let me forget 85 Palmeit.

prayers for india

These prayers follow a visit to India to see work done by Amos partners
with those rebuilding after the tsunami, and among the Dalit communities
working with the Tamarind Project. (Dalits are those formerly known as
'outcastes'.)

prayer following the tsunami wave

God our companion and our hope
We remember those who suffered through the tsunami wave —
A wave of destruction that took family and friends
Homes, boats and businesses.
A wave so shocking that people are still traumatized,
Memories still lost, communities still seeking to rebuild
    deeply shattered lives.

In their pain and suffering you were there in their rescuers
And beside them in their loss.
You were with them in their crucifixion
You are beside them in their slow journey to resurrection.
May tsunami victims find their future —
Find a way to go forward and rebuild
And be strengthened by the hope and liberation
Of the wounded God.

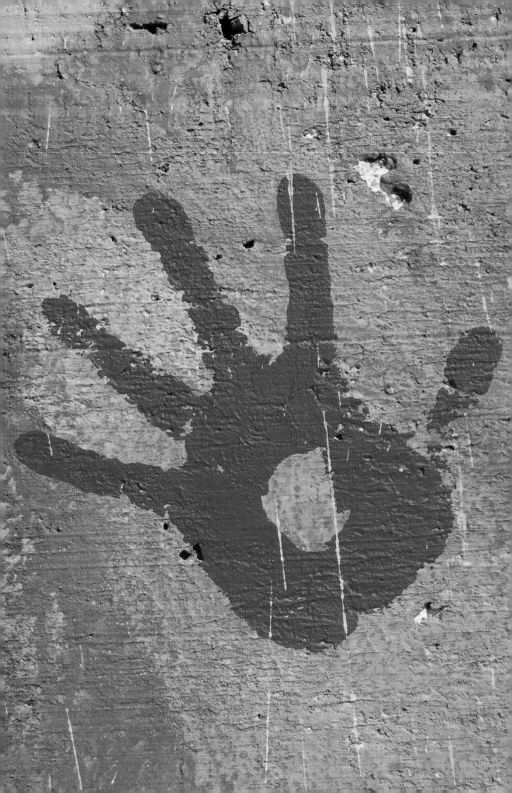

prayer for the dalits of india

Inclusive God — who values all equally
We pray for the Dalit community of India —
Over 200 million who are trapped by the caste system
And treated as 'outcaste'.
They have chosen the name 'Dalit' —
It means the 'crushed', 'broken' or 'oppressed'
And they are struggling to break free
From this tradition that would keep them captive.
They suffer abuse and daily attacks
And long to have the freedom envisaged by their champion —
Dr Ambedkar — who wrote the Indian Constitution
Which enshrines their rights.
Jesus, you break rules of caste and gender, race and religion
You are hope to the Dalits — a community so often ignored.
Your life and death remind us that all are valuable in God's eyes.
May Dalits find their liberation and dignity
Their freedom, their future and their hope.

Blessed

a prayer for a dalit village:
gomathimuthupuram in tamil nadu

Welcoming God, we pray for the people of Gomathimuthupuram —
It may be a hard name to pronounce
But it is a beautiful village — with beautiful trees
Where we received such a welcome
They danced, sang and prayed for us.
A village without a single vehicle —
Life revolving round St Stephen's Church.
Here we support the Tamarind Project
That helps young people get to school
And provides computer classes for all-age training
And supports a nearby orphanage.
The tamarind tree is deep-rooted and hardy
Providing in many ways for the people's needs
And it is beautiful —
So too are the people of Gomathimuthupuram
And we remember them today
And pray that the chains of caste will disappear
And that life will become easier
And that the seeds of hope that have been planted
Will come to fruition.

prayer about the wall of separation in a land once called holy

Living God, in Jesus you broke down the wall of division.
We see other walls that divide in our world
Like the separation wall that cuts into the heart of Palestine
Imprisoning a whole community —
Cutting them off from one another, from their work, from hospitals
From education and from places of worship.

God of liberation, strengthen them in their struggle
May hope be born again from the Prince of Peace's birthplace
   in Bethlehem
And throughout this land once called holy.

May Palestinians find justice at last
So Palestine and Israel can both live in peace —
Both live securely — both live in freedom
Without walls, without checkpoints, closures and curfews.
May we realize the great message of hope that all are chosen or none
We're all in this together —
One God, one community, one hope, one future.

prayer for nazareth:
town of the annunciation

O God, we pray for Nazareth — too often ignored —
Even guidebooks say 'do not bother to go'.
Can any good come from you we wonder?
Yet the angel Gabriel did not pass you by
He came and sought out Mary
Sought her out in this tiny insignificant town
And said 'Hail favoured one'
And so the whole wonderful liberation story begins
Not with the powerful and influential
Not with the rich or with celebrities
But here in an ordinary place — that is forever holy.
Thank you, God, that here a message burst
Unexpectantly upon a surprised young woman —
A message that must have been accompanied
By shame and misunderstanding
And yet . . . a message to have angels singing
Shepherds hurrying . . . and wise men wondering —
A message that still has the power
To plant a seed of hope in all of us —
That God is not far off — indeed much closer than we think —
Renewing our spirits — restoring our souls
And walking with us as we carry on living and telling the story.
So don't let us ignore Nazareth or pass it by
Because here our story begins.

prayer for avocado tree school in nicaragua

In a town called La Concepcion and known as La Concha
We find Avocado Tree School — it is a place of hope
In a town where 85 per cent are unemployed —
So in each family someone goes to Costa Rica
To try and earn a living and so families are split.
We pray, Lord, for Avocado Tree School in La Concha —
We thank you for dedicated teachers —
May they have patience working with the children —
Especially as the classes are so large.

Avocado is a place of so much potential —
So much hope — so much joy
The children long to learn — they are so motivated
We pray for them and for their future.
It costs so much to get to higher education and then . . .
There are no jobs except in sweatshops or by leaving the country
God of the just heart — touch our hearts so we don't forget
But keep on doing small deeds of beauty and care to support them.

We pray for jobs for the parents and healthcare for all
At a price that can be afforded.
They ask us to pressurize our government to stop raising
    the level of conflict in the world —
They say 'peace is what we need
So we can concentrate on fighting poverty'.
'War is raising the price of oil and that affects us all' —
'What seems like a small rise for your country is impossible for the
    poor to pay —
So we get poorer'.
God of the just heart — touch our hearts so we hear
So we remember and respond.
And thank you that in La Concha there is such a creative, hopeful place.

prayer for nicaragua:
a call for trade justice

O Nicaragua
You are a poem — you are a song
Like a primitive painting — so bright and so strong
You are a story — you are a prayer
You're the birth of a dream and we'll follow you there
You are bright colours and birds of all kinds
You're trees and you're flowers — you're everything fine.

O Nicaragua
You are a longing like an unspoken prayer
Where time holds its breath, you are joy and despair
O Nicaragua
Land of beauty — land of creativity
We meet your people
We hear your stories
We are inspired by your poetry, paintings, songs and theology.
Together may we learn to travel to justice for all
Particularly for the poor, the marginalized and the forgotten
As they battle against poverty.
If there were justice in World Trade
Nicaragua would stand a chance.
May we campaign for this with renewed energy as we remember
The struggling communities of this wonderful land.
O God, companion of the forgotten and champion of the ignored
Be our inspiration and our guide to show compassion.

prayer of blessing for travel

Living God, you walk beside us —
We pray for your blessing on those who travel at this time
May each one know your peace and the sense of your presence —
May they remember you are the God who travels with us
God of love and mercy, we pray for protection for travellers
And for a safe and speedy return
May they fear no evil and know no evil
Comfort them in the pain of separation from loved ones
Until they are united
Loving God — beside us on our journeys
We commend those who travel to your hands and your love
Until we meet again.

meditation for travellers trying to cope with stress at airports

God our companion — as we travel and as our friends travel
It can be a very stressful time —
With queue after queue and search after search
They say it is all for our safety — and so it is —
But who made us vulnerable and how?
So we grit our teeth and try to behave well
When we feel treated without respect — herded this way and that
I try to think of those for whom it is worse —
Palestinians who queue for hours at checkpoints
Then can be turned back, even with a permit, just on a whim.
I have freedom to travel — they do not.
I have choices but the poor and hungry and the homeless do not.
My only irritation is endless queues and waiting for baggage
I become impatient —
But then I think of asylum seekers and refugees and my moans stop.
I have such freedom even in these ludicrously bureaucratic
    and security-obsessed days.
I still have freedom and I cherish it and I long for others to share it —
And not to be kept in prison without trial
Not to be tortured to give us information
Not to be treated brutally and flown round the world
On 'extraordinary rendition' flights thus subcontracting the torture.

Not to have to risk their lives to get to a country
Where they can make a living.
So, Lord, when I am impatient at airports teach me to
   meditate and pray
For others and be more patient . . .
And maybe I should be at airports less now
Since flying causes such problems for our environment as well as
   my stress levels.

airport thoughts

I was at Miami Airport recently and saw that I must not say
Certain words — they are a security risk —
I cannot remember them all — but one was 'bomb' —
And I am happy not to say that.
But I do want to say certain words like 'human rights'
And 'justice' and 'peace'.
I do not want the word 'freedom' hijacked
As an excuse to use violence and to deprive others of their freedom —

So I want to say 'freedom' loudly
I do want to say 'love your neighbour'
And 'love your enemy'
And 'turn the other cheek'

And I do want to shout very loudly
'Do unto others as you would have them do to you'

Then I have nothing more to say.

chapter 3

---

seasonal prayers and prayers for special occasions

prayer for the new year

Ever-loving God, it is a new year full of new opportunities
As we ask forgiveness for the past
And make resolutions for the future
May we show your love and live your way

May we take time to pause and draw strength
And let our souls catch up
And be refreshed regularly through this year
May we show your love and live your way

May we remember the poor and the forgotten
The marginalized and the weak
And find ways to show your compassion
May we show your love and live your way

May the healing hope of the gospel be integral to our lives
So that the ways of justice and peace are reflected in us
May we show your love and live your way

May we take time to see the beauty of your world —
To see the beauty of trees, flowers, birds and animals —
To cherish them and work for the sustaining of our garden home —
So that we leave it in a good state for generations to come
May we show your love and live your way

May our hearts be refreshed by joy, music, creativity, love and hope
So we in turn can bring hope and joy to others.
Throughout this year
may we show your love and live your way.

palm sunday

Jesus, bringer of a new way to live
What a sign — riding in gently on a donkey
Welcomed as the Son of David
But he was the warrior king —
You refused a war horse and chose the donkey
You came in to Jerusalem as the peace king
Not really as a king — perhaps the prince of peace —
Olive branches symbolizing peace were waved before you
This is a new world order — not the power of weapons
But the power of love
Not one who conquers with violence
But one who sacrifices rather than defends himself
Jesus, bringer of a new way to live
You have given us a sign
And a way to follow
That heals and brings hope

prayer for easter: thinking of the church of the holy land

Ever-living God, in this time of Easter,
We ask that we will discover afresh the hope of the resurrection.
We are grateful for the Church that maintains its witness
In the pains and struggles of Palestine and Israel.
Thank you that even in these days of walking their Via Dolorosa
They have not forgotten the Easter message
 That burst from the tomb in Jerusalem
Spreading first around that land that once was holy
Then reaching out to the whole world.
Thank you that they have not let that flame die.
May we not forget them
And may our lives show the confidence
Of those who have also reached out
And touched the living God however tentatively
And though we may have been filled with doubts
In our times of darkness
May we catch a glimpse of a flicker of light —
That reminds us that we are always walking
Towards the dawn as we walk with you
And may our hearts expand with hope
As we sense the power and meaning of your resurrection.

prayer for st george's day

O God, the distant memory of the martyr St George
Can still inspire and challenge.
This saint from Palestine is still remembered across the Middle East
As the healer, as the green one who protects the environment —
He is respected across the faiths.
In England where he is our patron saint this encourages us
To better relationships with one another
To respect different viewpoints and faiths
And to look after this wonderful world we have been given.
It reminds us to love humanity and love our world.
O God, let the witness of a martyr
Who stands for the values of your community
Against the powerful empire of domination
Remind us of the journey we must take —
A journey showing compassion, mercy and justice to all
So that our world might be healed and brought back
From the ways of violence to the ways of wholeness.
May any ideas of excluding the other be removed
From our minds and lives
As we realize that in you, giving God
There is no scarcity of blessing —
We do not have to try and own you or define you.
You have already defined us by making us in your image
And by showing us the example of your vulnerable love.

prayer for the right use of the bible

Generous and loving God, whom we find in the pages of the Bible
May we understand who wrote it and why —
May we recognize how it has had a chequered past —
Inspiring so many and introducing so many to you and your character
And yet also regularly being used as a book of oppression —
Over 500 years ago in Latin America
In the apartheid days of South Africa
In the many attacks on Jewish communities in Europe over hundreds
    of years
In the oppression and removal of the Palestinian community from
    Palestine
It has been used to justify slavery
The oppression of women
And the oppression of gays and lesbians. So . .
May we be sensitive and responsible in our interpretation —
Reflecting the liberation, hope and love for all
That is also part of our great story —
Reflecting the wonderful message of the Sermon on the Mount —
Calling for love of neighbour and even love of enemy.
Bless those who try to make visible the ways of justice and peace
At the heart of its vision —
And to set the Bible free from being a book of oppression
Instead letting it be an uplifting book
Of dignity and resurrection
Of peacemaking and community building
Of salvation, renewal, wholeness and joy.
May we learn to love the Bible . . . but to be discerning —
Treating it with care so we reflect your liberating ways.

making holy dreams
come true
(a christmas prayer for bethlehem)

What have they done to the 'Little Town'?
Imprisoned it in a concrete wall
Bethlehem — once a holy city
Trapped inside a ghetto wall.
Here where angels sang of peace
Where love and hope were born anew
Once surrounded by a heavenly host
Now surrounded by a concrete view.

Yet people crushed and hidden away
Still celebrate on Christmas Eve
Lighting candles for the child —
They still remember — still believe.
So light a candle this Holy Night
For Bethlehem and Beit Sahour
And for all the people caught inside
That cold and grey prison wall.

Longing for a world of peace
Where all are treated equally
Where all can recognize their worth
Where all can live with dignity —
Where all can join hands with neighbours
Whether Muslim, Christian, Jew
And find a way to live together
Making holy dreams come true.

prayer for christmas eve

O God — Christmas Eve is such a wonderful time
Lights and laughter
Excitement and expectation
Candles and carols
Family and friends
Food and fun
And we try to stop to pray —
Or read a Christmas poem of John Betjeman
And I'm always moved as we come to those words
'And is it true ? And is it true . . .
The maker of the stars and sea
Become a child on earth for me?'
As he asserts that if this is so 'nothing can compare with this truth'
And I find it hard to carry on because there is nothing more to say
Because it reveals that you are the God
With such a precious love for humanity —
So we must cherish human rights
You are the God of humility — made visible in the ordinary person
In the everyday ordinariness of life
You are the God of the forgotten and insignificant — and therefore
   there is hope for all
And we too are shown how to live

And you are the God of Bethlehem today —
You would choose it again precisely because the world thinks it is
Insignificant and its people are of no value
So the angels would sing again to say 'here God is at home'

And the wise would be surprised again saying — 'here God is at home'
And shepherds, and carpenters making olive-wood gifts
And tour guides with no work, and drivers of coaches for pilgrims
And innkeepers and all the community — women, children and men —
Crushed, humiliated, invaded and imprisoned
Can stand up tall with confidence and proclaim 'here God is at home'
Because you have shown your character in Bethlehem —
You affirmed humanity in Bethlehem . . . and still do today
And that is the message of Christmas Eve.

prayer for peace in the wounded places

Vulnerable and wounded God —
We pray for peace in the wounded places of our world.
Some have problems so great that we are tempted to despair
And feel they can never be solved.

But may we never lose hope.
We are the community of resurrection
So lift our spirits — renew our vision
And particularly give us strength
To support the peacemakers in those places
That are suffering.

May we be those who refuse to walk by on the other side —
And be those who build links of love and support.

Vulnerable and wounded God
We pray for peace in the wounded places of our world.

meditation at the end of a holy land pilgrimage: forward to our galilee

We have journeyed in the footsteps of Jesus to Jerusalem, Bethlehem,
Nazareth, the Sea of Galilee and the Mount of Beatitudes.
Now as twenty-first century pilgrims we will probably fly home
From the smart new airport at Tel Aviv.
But what were the disciples told?
They were told that Jesus had gone ahead of them to Galilee.
It goes full circle — they are to go back to where they began —
They are to go home — there is work to be done
To carry on the work of Jesus and find Jesus there.

And wherever we return — it is our Galilee
Where we are called to be disciples
Where we are called to keep walking onwards
Where we will always find that Christ has gone before us
A peacemaker in a world that has no peace
A healer in a world that is broken
A saviour in a world that needs to be saved from its selfishness
Its pride, its violence and its greed.

Where we will find Jesus in the poor and the forgotten
We will find him in the breaking of the bread
So let us draw our strength — find our forgiveness —
Walk towards wholeness.
And though we may walk through valleys of despair
And through times of crucifixion
We are never without the resurrection hope
Because we are the community of hope
The community of love, the community of Jesus.

more holy dreams

God our friend and companion —
Each faith has a longing to follow you — to find the holy.
Each faith has some words close to the golden rule
That Jesus gave us —
'Do unto others as you would have them do to you'.
Each faith tries to deal with ego
So we learn to walk the humble road
And become better neighbours.
We have a dream — rooted in the scriptures
That mountains will be brought low and valleys lifted up —
That mountains of injustice, human rights abuse and oppression
Will be brought low so that a society of justice, humanity and caring
Will become a reality.
That instead of increasing the divisions and bitterness
We will see walls come down and neighbourliness increase
That hope will rise and peace will come
So arms sales fall and resources are shared
So all will see every human as equal
And treasure each one as made in the image of God
Then holy dreams will become true
And hope become a reality.

wednesdays on the wall

Ever-living and ever-loving God — here on London Wall —
Where hundreds of years ago
Symon the Anker prayed and wrote 'The Fruyte of Redempcyion' —
Here where, one hundred years ago
Samuel John Stone — hymn writer who wrote
'The Church's one foundation', wrote other hymns and poems —
Here as rector he prayed and cared
For the poorer workers of east London
And gave them shelter as they came into the City
Early to take advantage of cheaper trains.

Here in this beautiful but simple sacred space —
Praised by John Betjeman —
We have the humblest of services —
Yet we meet you in our liturgies
As we pray for those on our minds and in our hearts —
As we light our candles we place loved ones, friends, partners
Peacemakers and communities around the world into your hands.
We pray for justice and peace —
And we give thanks for times of joy and hope.

So on Wednesdays we touch the holy
And in a simple moment of quiet meet with you
And somehow life comes into perspective again.
So thank you, holy God, for this sacred space of prayer.

TEMPTATION RESTAURANT
- JERICHO -

SELF SERVICE
EAT AS MUCH AS YOU WANT

			US $
PRICE PER PERSON ONLY			
1. SOUP	ONE KIND		3.00
2. SALADS	ALL KINDS		7.00
3. MEAT	PLUS SALADS		11.00

EXTRA'S

1. SOFT DRINK		2.00
2. FRESH JUICE		2.00
3. COFFEE		2.00
4R. ORIENTAL SWEETS or CAKE		2.50
5. FRUIT SALAD		3.00
6. FRESH DATES		2.50

grace before a meal

God of the good gift
God of the generous heart
God revealed in the breaking of bread

It is good to pause before eating
So we do not take this meal for granted —
Thank you for the enjoyment of food and drink
Thank you for the fun and friendship of good company

With these gifts refresh us
And give us strength and generous hearts
To show your love and compassion —
So we give good gifts to others.

the god who dances

Henri Matisse is rumoured to have said
That he'd only believe in a God
Who understood how to dance.
I believe you are the God of dance —

You are the God who moves in creation
You are interwoven throughout evolution
You are the God who dances at dawn
You are the sparkle of light
You are the rhythm of life
Moving in mysterious ways

I feel you dancing on the earth
I sense your whisper in the trees
I breathe your spirit on the wind
You are the rhythm of life
Moving in mysterious ways

But always dancing
You are the God who dances.

prayer for forgiveness

O God, you see our motives and the desires of our hearts.
Forgive me for the mistakes I have made —
Forgive me for the wrong I have done —
Forgive me for walking the wrong way —
For not empathizing with that person —
For reacting too strongly.
Mistakes and failure make me feel I have lost my dignity
Restore my soul — make me whole
Give me back the spring in my step
The lightness in my heart
So I can bring hope and show love to others
And make good where I have made mistakes.
You are the God of second chances
Walk with me on the road back
To wholeness and dignity
To loving my neighbour and loving myself
And loving you with all my heart and soul.